IMAGES
of America

ELIZABETHTON

For Guy Burleson—a man who preserved the history of Elizabethton in word and deed.

IMAGES
of America

ELIZABETHTON

Michael and Lanette Depew

ARCADIA
PUBLISHING

Published by Arcadia Publishing
Charleston, South Carolina

Library of Congress Catalog Card Number: 2004109157

For all general information contact Arcadia Publishing at:
Telephone 843-853-2070
Fax 843-853-0044
E-mail sales@arcadiapublishing.com
For customer service and orders:
Toll-Free 1-888-313-2665

Visit us on the Internet at www.arcadiapublishing.com

HISTORIC LANDMARKS. The Doe River Covered Bridge (built 1882), the soldier's monument at Courthouse Square (built 1913), and Carter County Courthouse (built c. 1850), stand as a representation of the historical progression of Elizabethton and Carter County. (Photograph courtesy of Harold Lingerfelt.)

4

CONTENTS

ACKNOWLEDGMENTS

A very special thank you goes to the large number of people who guided us in our search for the photographs gathered in this collection. Not only did we come away with handfuls of photographs, but we also had the wonderful privilege of sharing in a bountiful supply of memories. It is our desire that, with the photographs gathered here, we can keep those memories of days gone by alive for years to come.

We would also like to thank Betty Depew and Lydia Depew for all of the long hours of babysitting Priscilla, Leo, Isaac and John. Without their help, we might have never finished this work.

And finally, Frank Merritt's two books *Later History of Carter County: 1865–1980* (Kingsport, TN: by the author, 1986) and *More History of Carter County* (Kingsport, TN: by the author, 1991), along with Rozella Hardin's book *From a Window on Hattie Avenue* (Johnson City, TN: by the author, 1993) proved to be invaluable to our research on Elizabethton.

ABOUT THE AUTHORS

Michael Depew has a bachelor's degree in philosophy and history from East Tennessee State University in Johnson City, Tennessee, and is completing a master's degree in history. He has taught U.S. History at East Tennessee State University and is a member of the Phi Alpha Theta History Honor Society.

Lanette Depew has a bachelor's degree in Elementary Education from Tennessee Temple University and has completed graduate work at East Tennessee State University. She has taught elementary and middle school at Tri-Cities Christian School in Johnson City, Tennessee, and is the author of *A Bridge Spanning Time*, a historical work of fiction about Elizabethton.

Both Michael and Lanette are members of the Watauga Historical Association and the Appalachian Writer's Association. They currently reside in Elizabethton, Tennessee, with their five children, Lydia, Priscilla, Leo, Isaac and John.

INTRODUCTION

Since Daniel Boone blazed the way across the Appalachian Mountains, Elizabethton, Tennessee, has been a place of beginnings and change. The settlers of the Watauga Valley, who were not afraid to strike out on their own, developed a new government autonomous from the colonies and the Crown in 1772 and purchased land directly from the Cherokee Indians in 1775. Once the settlement was established, frontiersmen including James Robertson, John Sevier, and John Carter along with the growing number of settlers worked hard to keep it thriving, even resisting an attack by Cherokee Chief "Old Abram" and his band of warriors at Fort Watauga in 1776.

In 1780, around the time John and Landon Carter finished their fine mansion near the Watauga River, men ready to defend the settlements west of the Appalachian Mountains mustered at Fort Watauga before traveling to King's Mountain, South Carolina, to defeat Major Ferguson. The battle that followed was a success for the Patriot cause, and was considered by some as a turning point of the Revolutionary War.

In 1796, the same year Tennessee was admitted into the Union, Carter County, named for Landon Carter, was created. Elizabethton, named for Landon's wife, Elizabeth MacLin Carter, was formed just a few years later in 1799. From then on, the town was well on its way to developing into a tight-knit community east of the Doe River. Nothing could have prepared it for the division of families (including the Carter family), neighborhoods, and churches brought about by the Civil War in the 1860s.

However, time healed most wounds, and by the early 1880s, the citizens worked together to construct a covered bridge that provided access to the train station and acres of farm land west of the Doe River. Houses and businesses built by visionary town builders Dr. Abraham Jobe, William P. Dungan, Dr. E.E. Hunter, and L.H. Rhudy were among the first new buildings to ornament the New Town once the covered bridge was finished. A mill race channeled from the Doe River along with the Watauga River remained the driving forces behind many different industries such as the Doe River Woolen Mill and the Doe River Overall Factory during the late 1800s and early 1900s. In 1912, the construction of the Wilbur Dam flooded Elizabethton with "light and power" causing many industries such as the Line and Twine and the Tennessee Cotton Mill to install electric motors. German-owned American Bemberg Corporation and its affiliate American Glanzstoff Corporation (later known as North American Rayon) began spinning artificial silk and rayon along the Watauga River in the late 1920s, impacting the community for much of the 20th century. Banks, drugstores, clothiers, and movie theatres emerged on Elk Avenue, efficiently utilizing this main thoroughfare of Elizabethton—despite the two world wars and depression that caused anguish in the community as well as across the nation.

Today, after nearly a century of operation, several industries including Bemberg and North American Rayon, with their towering brick smokestacks, distinct odor, and humming machinery, are just a memory, but Elizabethton continues to thrive. Downtown is still a commercial success even with the addition of several larger businesses in the area. The Chamber of Commerce along with the newly developed Downtown Association of Businesses organizes festivals and antique car drive-ins that remind one of the days of old. *The Wataugans*, the official outdoor drama of Tennessee, perform at the reconstructed Fort Watauga during the final three weeks of July and re-create the Revolutionary War incidents that helped develop our nation. Covered Bridge Days, held during the first week in June, celebrates the covered bridge, affectionately known as the "Queen of the Doe."

One

OLD TOWN/NEW TOWN

THE SNYDER HOUSE. Owned and operated by Henry H. Snyder, the Snyder House was the first hotel in Elizabethton. The dwelling, consisting of four large houses connected by passageways, was located at the intersection of Main and First Streets and was the hub of activity in Old Town Elizabethton from around 1850 to the early 1900s. (Photograph from the Murrell Family Collection, courtesy of the Archives of Appalachia.)

THE CARTER MANSION. Built by John Carter and his son Landon between 1775 and 1780, the Carter Mansion is considered the oldest frame house in Tennessee. The massive structure located east of town on the Watauga River reveals a touch of "wilderness elegance" with its hand hewn panels, crown molding, and two murals that have survived over the years. Several outbuildings such as servant's quarters, a blacksmith's shop, and even a slaughter house had, in the past, adorned the property that is now owned and maintained by the Tennessee Department of Environment and Conservation. (Photograph from the collection of the late W.G. Ziletti, courtesy of Joe Alexander.)

THE CARTER FAMILY FUNERARY MONUMENT. John Carter moved into the Watauga Valley during the early 1770s following a raid by the Shawnee Indians that looted his trading post in Carter's Valley. He served as chairman of the court of the Watauga Association, which was formed in 1772, and acted as representative from the Washington District to the North Carolina Assembly. After purchasing 640 acres of land along the Watauga River, John built his elaborate mansion with son Landon before dying of smallpox in 1781. (Photograph by authors.)

10

LANDON CARTER. Like his father, Landon Carter also served as a representative from the Washington District to the North Carolina Assembly as well as the Secretary of State for the State of Franklin. He and his wife, Elizabeth MacLin Carter, for whom Elizabethton was named, raised their family in the Carter Mansion. (Photograph by the authors.)

ALFRED MOORE CARTER. Alfred Moore Carter, eldest son of Landon and Elizabeth Carter, was a planter, merchant, iron master, and public official. He served as the first circuit court clerk of Carter County from 1810 to 1836. (Photograph originally printed in the *Watauga Spinnerette*, January/February 1954.)

THE ALFRED MOORE CARTER HOME. The Alfred Moore Carter Home is located on East Elk Avenue, which was regarded as Forge Street for a time. (Photograph originally printed in the *Watauga Spinnerette*, January/February 1954.)

CARTER FAMILY CEMETERY. John, Landon, Elizabeth, and their children are buried in the cemetery located on the grounds of the Carter Mansion. (Photograph by authors.)

ADMIRAL SAMUEL P. CARTER. S.P. Carter, eldest son of Alfred Moore Carter, was a naval officer who was given an army commission in the Union Army as brigadier general during the Civil War. He is the only American military person to have held the ranks of both brigadier general and naval admiral at the time of his retirement. (Photograph originally printed in the *Watauga Spinnerette*, January/February 1954.)

13

THE DOE RIVER FROM ELK AVENUE BRIDGE. This photograph, taken during the early 1900s from the bridge on Elk Avenue, shows the Doe River, houses along Academy Street, the Northern Methodist Church (sold in 1913 to Elizabethton First Free Will Baptist Church), and "the Crossover." Prior to the completion of the covered bridge, wagons and men on horseback used to ford the turbulent Doe River near this site. It is reported that, up until a recent flood, wagon ruts were still visible in the packed earth. (Photograph courtesy of Nancy Jane Earnest and Benjamin F. Earnest Jr.)

CARTER COUNTY COURTHOUSE. Built during the 1850s, the massive Carter County Courthouse has for more than a century represented the whole of Carter County, which extends far into the mountains. (Photograph courtesy of the city of Elizabethton.)

14

DUFFIELD ACADEMY. The Duffield Academy, the first school in Elizabethton, was erected near the Doe River during the early 1800s. Named for George Duffield, the academy was an all-male school until females were admitted in 1853. Through the years Duffield Academy has served several different schools, including a private school operated by the Presbyterian Church named Davies Academy and an elementary school in the Elizabethton City School System. The original building of the Duffield Academy was torn down in 1838, but its replacement, located only a few yards away, houses the administration building of the Carter County Schools. (Photograph by authors.)

THE OLD GIRLS' ACADEMY. An academy for girls, also located in Old Town on South Main Street, was organized during the 1830s. (Photograph by authors.)

THE DOE RIVER INN. Located on Academy Street in Old Town, the Old Arnett House (now the Doe River Inn) was built in the late 1800s. Christopher Arnett, owner of the house from around 1918, was known to cut hair on the front porch. Patrons brought their own haircutting stool. (Photograph by authors.)

THE DOE RIVER COVERED BRIDGE. Built in 1882, the Doe River Covered Bridge provided Old Town Elizabethton with access to the train station and farmland west of the Doe River. The bridge also offered a way of escape when the Watauga and Doe Rivers flooded the area in May 1901. Note the Range House (for a time known as the Jobe House) on the corner of Hattie Avenue and Riverside Drive; the house was built by Dr. Abraham Jobe during the late 1800s. (Photograph by authors.)

16

NEW TOWN ELIZABETHTON. Several residents of New Town are shaded by the trees that line Elk Avenue. Upon completion of the covered bridge, the citizens of Elizabethton began to fill the fields west of the Doe River with beautiful houses and successful businesses. The symmetry of the buildings and the width of Elk Avenue indicate a well-planned community. (Photograph courtesy of the city of Elizabethton.)

THE DUNGAN HOUSE. Built by Judge William P. Dungan in 1892, this house was the first in New Town Elizabethton to have electric, telephone, and water service. Judge Dungan served as judge and mayor of Elizabethton and was instrumental in establishing several organizations such as the People's Bank, Standard Grocery Company, and the Lynnwood Hotel. (Photograph from the collection of the late W.G. Ziletti, courtesy of Joe Alexander.)

ELK AVENUE. Water pipes were installed in Elk Avenue during the early 1900s. Note the steeple of First Baptist Church. Following the flood in May 1901, the church building was moved from Broad Street to the corner of Elk Avenue and Sycamore Street. (Photograph from the collection of the late W.G. Ziletti, courtesy of Joe Alexander.)

POSTCARD OF ELK AVENUE. The illustration on this postcard, postmarked 1913, shows downtown Elizabethton as it developed into a small city. Note the electrical lines powered by the Wilbur Dam built in 1910–1912. (Postcard from the collection of the late W.G. Ziletti, courtesy of Joe Alexander.)

18

FOURTH OF JULY PARADE, EARLY 1900S. Citizens of Elizabethton proudly pose in one of the first of many parades down Elk Avenue. (Photograph from the collection of the late W.G. Ziletti, courtesy of Joe Alexander.)

TAYLOR AT SYCAMORE SHOALS. This photograph of Gov. Bob Taylor speaking at Sycamore Shoals was taken by Samuel B. Walker and donated to the Archives of Appalachia in 1926. (Photograph from the collection of Mae Walker, courtesy of the Archives of Appalachia.)

F STREET, 1910. Residents walk along paved sidewalks near F Street of New Town Elizabethton. (Photograph courtesy of Nancy Jane Earnest and Benjamin F. Earnest Jr.)

POSTCARD OF ELIZABETHTON, POSTMARKED 1908. The photograph on this postcard, taken from Lynn Mountain, shows how quickly Elizabethton developed on the west side of the Doe River in the few years following the construction of the covered bridge. (Postcard courtesy of Nancy Jane Earnest and Benjamin F. Earnest Jr.)

20

Two

CITY OF POWER

ELK AVENUE BRIDGE AT THE TURN OF THE CENTURY. Elizabethton took pride in offering electricity to her residents following the completion of the Wilbur Dam in 1912. The "City of Power" sign presented by the Watauga Power Company began illuminating Elk Avenue Bridge in 1914. (Photograph courtesy of the City of Elizabethton.)

WATAUGA RIVER, EARLY 1900S. Throughout the late 1800s and early 1900s, numerous mills and factories derived their energy from the Watauga and Doe Rivers as well as from several creeks, tributaries, and mill runs. (Photograph courtesy of Guy Burleson.)

WILBUR DAM. Completed in 1912, the Wilbur Dam (also known as the Horseshoe Dam) was the first hydro-electric dam in Tennessee. The concrete structure, located on the Watauga River, 300 feet long, 55 feet high, and 58 feet wide at its base. (Photograph courtesy of Jim and Conni Vaughn.)

THE DOE RIVER COVERED BRIDGE. A mill race, channeled from the Doe River, remained the driving force behind many different industries during the late 1800s and early 1900s. Notice the absence of bars in the windows of the covered bridge. (Photograph courtesy of Jim and Connie Vaughn.)

THE DOE RIVER MILL RACE. The stream in the mill race travels through north Elizabethton before emptying into the Watauga River. (Photograph from the collection of the late W.G. Ziletti, courtesy of Joe Alexander.)

PANORAMIC VIEW OF ELIZABETHTON. Taken of the lower end of the Nat T. Perry property, this panoramic view shows Elizabethton from Sunset Hill. Note the factory in the background. The Watauga and Doe Rivers and the mill race on the Doe River ran through the northern part of town, providing energy to several industries like the Doe River Overall Factory and the Doe River Woolen Mills. (Photograph courtesy of Nancy Jane Earnest and Benjamin F. Earnest Jr.)

THE TENNESSEE LINE AND TWINE. Established in the 1890s by M.E. Clark and Julian Crandell, the Tennessee Line and Twine is Elizabethton's oldest industry. The business, which merged with the Tennessee Cotton Mill in the late 1800s, extended 735 feet down Lynn Avenue to Roan Street and continued operation until 1971. (Photograph courtesy of the City of Elizabethton.)

24

AERIAL SHOT OF NORTH AMERICAN RAYON AND BEMBERG. American Glanzstoff Corporation, later known as North American Rayon Corporation (foreground), along with its affiliate American Bemberg Corporation (upper right), operated throughout much of the 1900s. The two companies offered a wide range of resources for employees and their families, such as company housing, recreational opportunities, and an informative publication called the *Watauga Spinnerette*. (Photograph from the collection of the late W.G. Ziletti, courtesy of Joe Alexander.)

BEMBERG. American Bemberg Corporation began spinning artificial silk along the Watauga on October 29, 1926 and continued until December 19, 1970. (Photograph from the collection of the late W.G. Ziletti, courtesy of Joe Alexander.)

ELK AVENUE. The presence of the Soldiers' Monument just past Elk Avenue Bridge dates this popular photograph of Elk Avenue to about 1913. Note the Grand Theatre on the right. (Photograph from the collection of the late W.G. Ziletti, courtesy of Joe Alexander.)

ELK AVENUE STORE. This photograph of the Elk Avenue Store on the corner of Elk Avenue and Sycamore Street was taken around the 1920s. Note the posters on the windows advertising the Ringling Bros. Circus. (Photograph courtesy of Guy Burleson.)

FOUR WAY SERVICE STATION. B.A. Brown and Gene Chambers operated the Four Way Service Station, located on the intersection of Elk Avenue and Broad Street, from the late 1930s to the early 1970s. (Photograph courtesy of Richard and Phyllis Lovette.)

THE LYNNWOOD HOTEL. Built along the Doe River with a view of Lynn Mountain, the Lynnwood Hotel (also, for a short period, called the Governor Taylor Hotel) offered a respite for travelers as well as a source of entertainment for the citizens of Elizabethton for nearly 70 years. The building at one time or another boasted 35 rooms, a ballroom, and a bowling alley. It was the site of many political speeches, fund-raisers, and parties. (Photograph courtesy of the city of Elizabethton.)

IN THE HEART OF THE ALLEGHENIES. An old Lynnwood advertisement summoning vacationers to a "Summer in the Mountains" promises hot and cold running water, telephone and electric lights in every room, and steam heat. (Photograph courtesy of City of Elizabethton; Advertisement courtesy of Harold Lingerfelt.)

TAYLOR DRUGS. Dr. S.O. Powers and Dr. Allen Taylor stand among the men in this photograph of Taylor Drugs taken during the 1930s. Taylor Drug Company was incorporated in January 1926. (Photograph courtesy of Harold Lingerfelt.)

BURGIE DRUGS. This photograph of Burgie Drugs, taken in the 1930s, shows Harry Burgie who worked as a druggist in Elizabethton for 52 years before his death in August 1951. The grand opening of Larry Proffitt's Burgie Drugs on West G Street in 1976 preserved many of the fixtures of the original business as well as the spirit that has served Elizabethton since 1892. (Photograph courtesy of Harold Lingerfelt.)

BURGIE DRUGS. The pharmacist's licenses of Harry Burgie hang above the counter of Burgie Drugs to this day. When Harry first began his practice in 1892, Tennessee law did not require pharmacists to be licensed. His first license, which he received in the late 1890s, was the 12th license issued in Tennessee. The license pictured here is actually Harry's second one, as the first was too fragile to remove from the frame. (Pharmacy license courtesy of Larry Proffitt.)

BURGIE DRUGS, 1967. "Soda jerks" Lynn Smith and David Shouse work at the soda fountain at Burgie Drugs. (Photograph courtesy of Larry Proffitt.)

MAX JETT. Max Jett, who owned Burgie Drugs from Harry Burgie's retirement until 1971, poses with Gov. Frank G. Clement. (Photograph courtesy of Larry Proffitt.)

HALE'S DRUGS. Dr. T.J. Hale Sr. worked for City Drugs before purchasing Central Drug Store with Dr. W.G. Frost in the 1940s. Notice the presence of the Parks-Belk building. (Photograph courtesy of Jeter and Phyllis Hale.)

HALE'S DRUGS. Young Jeter Hale rides his horse into his father's drugstore to get an ice cream cone during a parade. Note the presence of Jay Fleenor's Insurance Office across the street. (Photograph courtesy of Jeter and Phyllis Hale.)

HALE'S DRUGS, 1950S. Dr. T.J. Hale Sr. poses with Bill Bellamy, manager of Parks-Belk. (Photograph courtesy of Jeter and Phyllis Hale.)

HALE'S DRUGS, 1960s. Dr. T.J. Hale Sr. and Hazel Hale stand in front of Hale's Drugs. (Photograph courtesy of Jeter and Phyllis Hale.)

TAYLOR SNACK BAR. Dr. S.O. Powers, longtime partner of Dr. Allen F. Taylor, bought Taylor's interest in Taylor's Drug Store in February 1951. (Photograph courtesy of Harold Lingerfelt.)

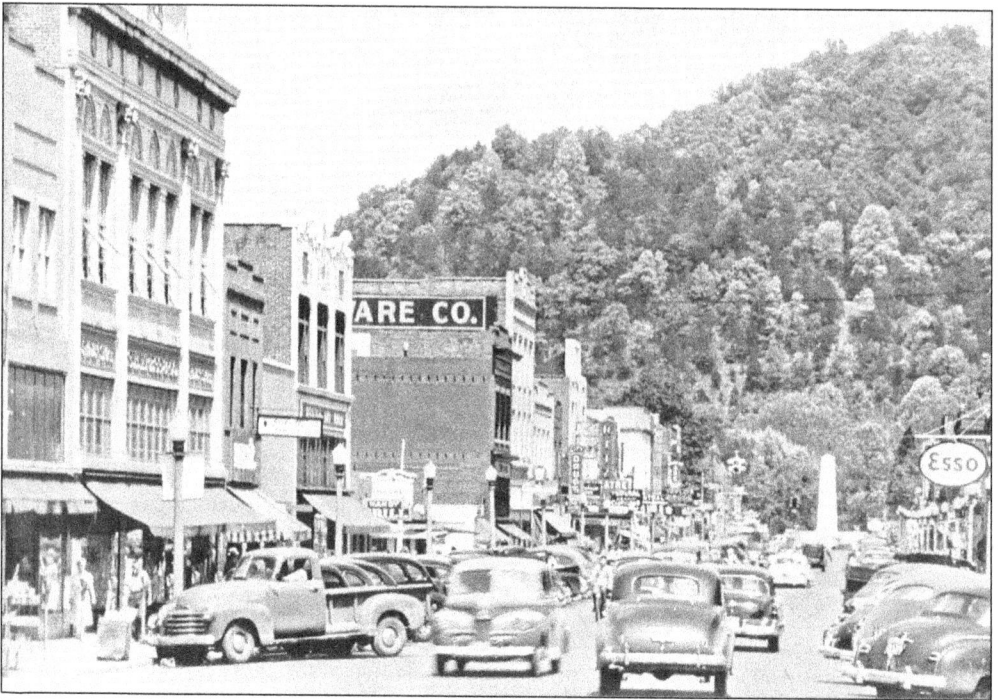

ELK AVENUE. Industries like the Tennessee Chair Company, American Bemberg Corporation, and American Glanzstoff Corporation contributed to the commercial success of downtown Elizabethton in the 1930s, 1940s, and 1950s. Note the two-way traffic. The business streets became one-way in 1952. (Photograph courtesy of the City of Elizabethton.)

RITZ THEATRE. This close-up view of the above photograph shows three of the numerous drugstores of downtown as well as Federal Clothiers and the Ritz Theatre. (Photograph courtesy of the city of Elizabethton.)

H.M. Slagle & Sons. Stores in the downtown area such as the Men's Clothing Store of H.M. Slagle Sr. provided goods and services for the growing community. "Slagle's" began operation in 1907 and ran successfully for 48 years. (Top photograph courtesy of John and Pam Huber, bottom photograph courtesy of Guy Burleson.)

S.H. KRESS COMPANY. Managed by J.H. Hunt, S.H. Kress Company formally opened its doors December 1929 with 50 salesladies and 7 salesmen. (Photograph from the collection of the late W.G. Ziletti, courtesy of Joe Alexander.)

S.H. KRESS COMPANY. When S.H. Kress Company became part of Elk Avenue in the late 1920s, it was one of America's largest chain stores. The "five and dime" served Elizabethton for nearly 50 years before closing on January 31, 1978. (Photograph from the collection of the late W.G. Ziletti, courtesy of Joe Alexander.)

36

DOWNTOWN POSTCARDS OF ELK AVENUE. A comparison of these two postcards reveals the subtle changes that took place in downtown Elizabethton between the 1950s and 1970s. (Postcards from the collection of the late W.G. Ziletti, courtesy of Joe Alexander.)

CONCRETE AWNINGS. With the addition of the awnings installed along Elk Avenue around 1978, the sidewalks were expanded 10 feet to allow for more pedestrian traffic. (Photographs courtesy of Harold Lingerfelt.)

CONCRETE AWNINGS. The concrete awnings were specially designed for Elizabethton by Frank Knisley. (Top photograph courtesy of Harold Lingerfelt, bottom photograph from the collection of the late W.G. Ziletti, courtesy of Joe Alexander.)

HAROLD LINGERFELT, 1965. Using his speed-graphics camera, Harold Lingerfelt took photographs for his monthly health column and of newlywed couples and contest winners to be put in the *Elizabethton Star*. Harold, who purchased Taylor Drug Store with Robert M. Little in 1963, also served as mayor of Elizabethton from 1988 to 1996. (Photograph courtesy of Harold Lingerfelt.)

LINGERFELT PHARMACY. Employees of Lingerfelt Pharmacy during the late 1960s are (seated) Sheila Street, Dot Kimbrell, Viola Lingerfelt, and Leta Hale; (standing) Richard Tittle, Mark Lingerfelt, and Harold Lingerfelt. (Photograph courtesy of Harold Lingerfelt.)

MONROE BARNS. Harold Lingerfelt skillfully communicates with deaf patron Monroe Barns. Monroe attended Tennessee School for the Deaf and was proficient at playing the trumpet. (Photograph courtesy of Harold Lingerfelt.)

41

THE BONNIE KATE THEATRE. The Bonnie Kate Theatre was designed by J. Frank Spires, an architect from Welch, West Virginia, and built by Roy Trump. The theatre opened the week of May 16, 1926 with 500 seats. Ernest Wilcox was the theatre's first projectionist. Advertised in the late 1960s as the Rocking Chair Theatre, the Bonnie Kate theatre was the first theatre east of the Mississippi River to have rocking chair seating. (Photograph courtesy of Leroy Policky.)

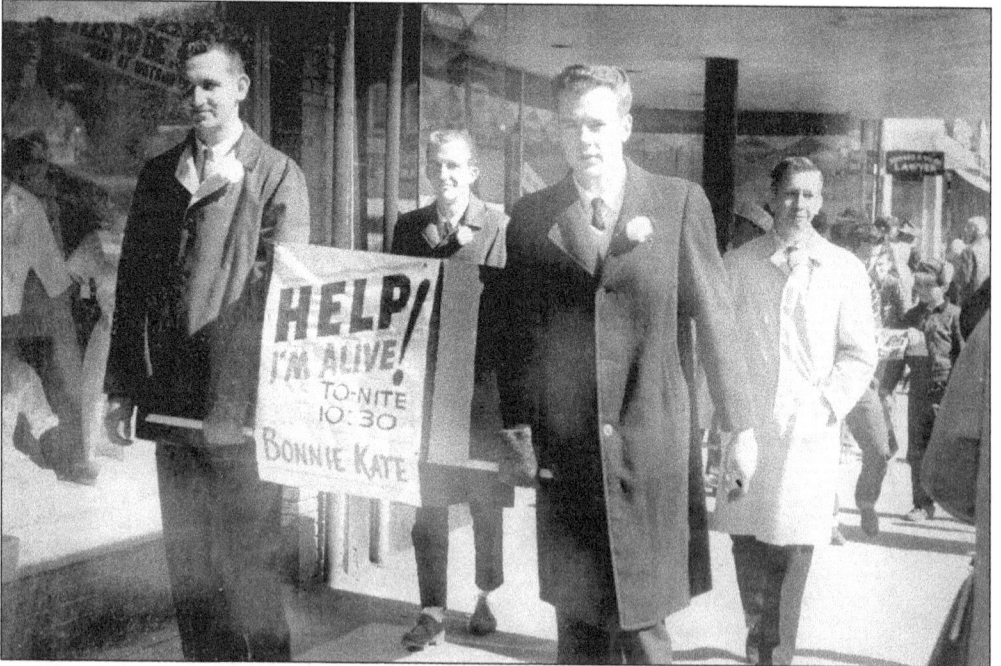

BURIED ALIVE. "Pallbearers" walk through town advertising for the Bonnie Kate Theatre. (Photograph courtesy of Leroy Policky.)

THE BONNIE KATE THEATRE. In 1955, Audie Murphy's autobiographical film, *To Hell and Back*, came to the Bonnie Kate. True to the showmanship of the day, the owner convinced the National Guard to bring one of the tanks from their unit to help publicize the film. (Photograph courtesy of Leroy Policky.)

THE BONNIE KATE THEATRE. The marquee of the grand Bonnie Kate Theatre was replaced during the holiday season of December 1964 and January 1965. (Photograph courtesy of Leroy Policky.)

THE ELIZABETHTON STAR. Benjie Earnest, carrier for the *Elizabethton Star*, delivers papers to residents in 1957. (Photograph courtesy of Nancy Jane Earnest and Benjamin F. Earnest Jr.)

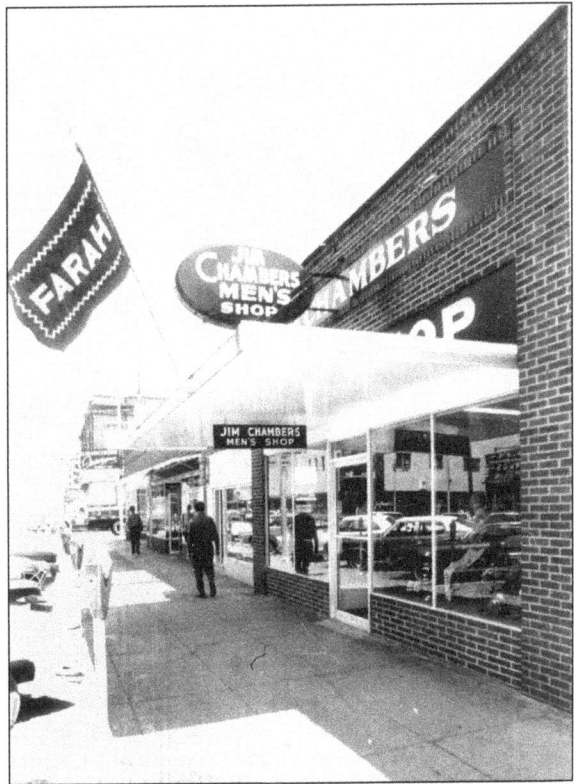

JIM CHAMBERS' MEN'S SHOP, 1960S.
For 30 years, Jim G. Chambers,
pictured with his son, Jim W.
Chambers, owned and operated
his shop until his death in 1979.
(Photographs courtesy of Jim and
Kay Chambers.)

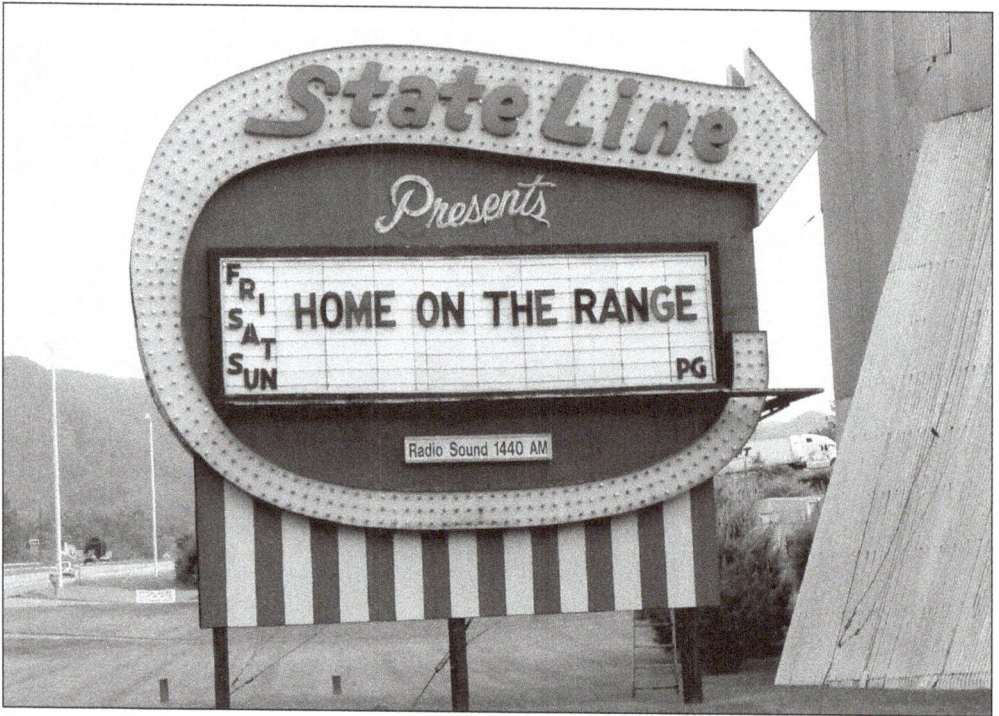

STATELINE DRIVE-IN. Since 1947, Stateline Drive-In has offered feature films to the community. The theatre is still in operation from April to September with FM, AM, and speaker sound. (Photograph by authors.)

SAMMONS' TOY FAIR AND THE "HOLE IN THE WALL." Richard Sammons and his mother, Myrtle, stand in front of Sammons' Toy Fair in this photograph taken in 1969. The walk up window located on the left of the building was known as the "Hole in the Wall" and was famous for its hot dogs and quick service. (Photograph courtesy of Richard Sammons.)

DAIRY QUEEN. Founded by Mark and Martha McElroy in 1950, the restaurant known as the Betsy Dairy Creme began as a Dairy Queen. Mike Honeycutt and Patricia Townsend are serving a customer in this photograph dated June 1968. (Photograph courtesy of Teresa Isaacs Caldwell.)

DAIRY KREME. In 1965, Wayne and Ruth Isaacs purchased the Dairy Queen located on the corner of F Street and Lynn Avenue. Mr. Isaacs changed the name of the restaurant to Wayne's Dairy Kreme in 1976. (Photograph courtesy of Teresa Isaacs Caldwell.)

RIDGEWOOD BARBECUE. Owned and operated by the Proffitt Family, Ridgewood Barbecue has provided the community with its beef and pork barbecue seasoned with Mrs. Grace Proffitt's secret sauce since 1948. (Photograph courtesy of Ridgewood Barbecue.)

RIDGEWOOD BARBECUE. Lisa Proffitt Peters carries on the tradition of serving delicious barbecue with her husband, Mark. (Photograph courtesy of Ridgewood Barbecue.)

RIDGEWOOD BARBECUE. Pictured here is one of the old menus at Ridgewood offering a "homemade sauce that's different." (Menu courtesy of Ridgewood Barbecue.)

Menu

Ridgewood Grill

Telephone Dial 2941, Bluff City

Sandwiches and Breakfasts

Special Bar-Becue Pork Sandwich with a home made sauce that's different			50c
with French Fries			65c
Delicious Country Ham Sandwich			75c
Tenderloin Sandwich			75c

Hot Dogs	15c	Egg with Lettuce and Tomato	25c
Hamburger	25c	Lettuce and Tomato	20c
Cheeseburger	30c	Pork Chop	45c
Bacon and Tomato	35c	Toasted Cheese	25c
Bacon and Egg	45c	Egg and Cheese	30c
Grilled Cheese	25c	Home Made Pimento Cheese	30c
Baked Ham	45c	Fish Sandwich	25c

Any Sandwich without Lettuce and Tomato 5c Less
Sandwiches served with ½ portion of French Fries 15c extra

Oyster Stew (in season)	65c
French Fries	25c
All Soups	30c
Chili	30c

―――――o―――――

BREAKFAST

Country Ham and Eggs		$1.25
Sugar Cured Ham and Eggs		85c
Bacon and Eggs		60c
Sausage and Eggs		65c
Pie		15c
Coffee	5c; On Curb	10c
Sweet Milk		10c
Butter Milk		10c
All Cold Drinks in Dining Room or on Curb		10c
Juices		15c

DINO'S RESTAURANT. In 1963, Dino Senesi opened a new restaurant on Elk Avenue. Through the years, Dino's Italian menu has become a favorite in Elizabethton. (Photograph by authors.)

CARTER COUNTY
HISTORIC MARKER
JUNE 20 1963
- -
FIRST LASAGNA SERVED
IN EAST TENNESSEE

DINO'S RESTAURANT. Even though some have questioned the historical accuracy of Dino's "historic marker," the first lasagna served in East Tennessee—by Dino—was, in fact, in 1963. (Photograph by authors.)

DINO'S RESTAURANT. Dino is pictured here with Bill Wade, quarterback for the Chicago Bears. (Photograph courtesy of Dino's Restaurant.)

JACK AND DOROTHY COFFMAN. The Southern Restaurant, located on Elk Avenue, was opened by Jack and Dorothy Coffman in 1948. (Photograph courtesy of Joe Coffman.)

SOUTHERN RESTAURANT, 1940S. Ethel Moreland and Thelma Dunn are among the women pictured in this photograph of the Southern Restaurant. (Photograph courtesy of Joe Coffman.)

SOUTHERN RESTAURANT, APRIL 1958. Joe Coffman celebrates his first birthday with (seated) Vicky Webb, Jamie Browning, and Dottie Brookshire; (standing) Eddie Edens, Charles Coffman, and Bill Armstrong. (Photograph courtesy of Joe Coffman.)

WESTWAY DRIVE-IN, 1959. Cheerleaders pose in front of Westway Drive-In, which was located on W. Elk Avenue. (Photograph courtesy of Jeter and Phyllis Hale.)

SOLDIERS' MONUMENT AND OLD TOWN ELIZABETHTON. This photograph of Old Town Elizabethton shows a busy part of town in the 1930s regardless of the city's expansion across the Doe River. (Photograph courtesy of the City of Elizabethton.)

Three

ELIZABETHTON LIFE

OUR GANG, c. 1946. Included in this group of boys preparing to go to camp in Unicoi are Bill Gentry, Danny McCall, Floyd "Meatball" Corrnett, Don Blevins, Buzz Guess, Ischmel Bishop, Paul Lewis, "Bo" Campbell, Bill Markland, Baldy Corrnett, Jerry Hensley, Ken Bishop, Harold Bishop, Sherrill Heaton, Jack Kent, Bill Perry, Mark Fair, Eddie Sturgill, James Armstrong, Ralph Bowers, Randy Scalf, Toby Johnson, Jimmy Bishop, Pete Johnson, Joe Spitzer, and Nick Hyder. (Photograph courtesy of Richard and Phyllis Lovette.)

TWEETSIE. For more than 60 years (from 1881 to 1950) the East Tennessee and Western North Carolina Railroad, affectionately known as "Tweetsie," connected Elizabethton with Johnson City, Hampton, Cranberry, and Boone. Lumber, ore, coal, tobacco, and other resources were shipped out of the mountains as well as passengers, who visited nearby cities and picnicked in the Doe River Gorge. (Photograph courtesy of Guy Burleson.)

STATELINE DEPOT. Stateline Depot, located on the corner of Johnson Avenue and State Line Road, was one of many depots along the route. (Photograph courtesy of Lois Milhorn.)

NAT T. PERRY FAMILY. The East Tennessee and Western North Carolina Railroad was primarily built to accommodate the vast lumber, ore, coal, and tobacco industries; yet families also traveled through the cool tunnels and deep gorges of the "narrow gauge." (Photograph courtesy of Nancy Jane Earnest and Benjamin F. Earnest Jr.)

PICNIC AT PARDEE POINT. Hazel Perry Shepherd, Donna Perry Netherland, and Nat T. Perry picnic at Pardee Point after riding the "narrow gauge" into the Doe River Gorge in this photograph taken in the early 1900s. (Photograph courtesy of Nancy Jane Earnest and Benjamin F. Earnest Jr.)

DOE RIVER AND ET&WNC RAILROAD. The East Tennessee and Western North Carolina Railroad runs parallel to the Doe River in this photograph taken in the late 1800s. Time and flooding have since displaced most of the tracks along the line, but memories of Tweetsie will never grow dim. (Photograph courtesy of Guy Burleson.)

SWINGING BRIDGE, LATE 1930s. Conley H. Estep and Hattie E. Hyder Estep cross the swinging bridge which extended over the Watauga River near Wilbur Dam. Note the path that leads to the old Baptist church in the background. (Photograph courtesy of Jim and Connie Vaughn.)

ELIZABETHTON CITY BAND, c. 1910. The members of the Elizabethton City Band are, from left to right, the following: (front row) Sam Fondren, Murry Folsom, Stanley Greg, Director Ringling, Bob Donnley, Lynn Folson, and Maidson Folsom (sub for Bob Johnson); (back row) Joe Ferguson, Chester Edens, Taylor Morill, Drew Tipton, Paul Hendrickson, and Harry Hathaway (missing). (Photograph courtesy of Richard and Phyllis Lovette.)

FOURTH OF JULY PARADE, 1914. This photograph of a Fourth of July float traveling down F Street toward the intersection of F and Lynn Avenue was taken from the Nat T. Perry home, present site of First Baptist Church. (Photograph courtesy of Nancy Jane Earnest and Benjamin F. Earnest Jr.)

SUNSET HILL. Helen Jane Perry and James Jackson Perry proudly pose on their front gate in this photograph taken on the Nat T. Perry property at the corner of F Street and Lynn Avenue, c. 1915. (Photograph courtesy of Nancy Jane Earnest and Benjamin F. Earnest Jr.)

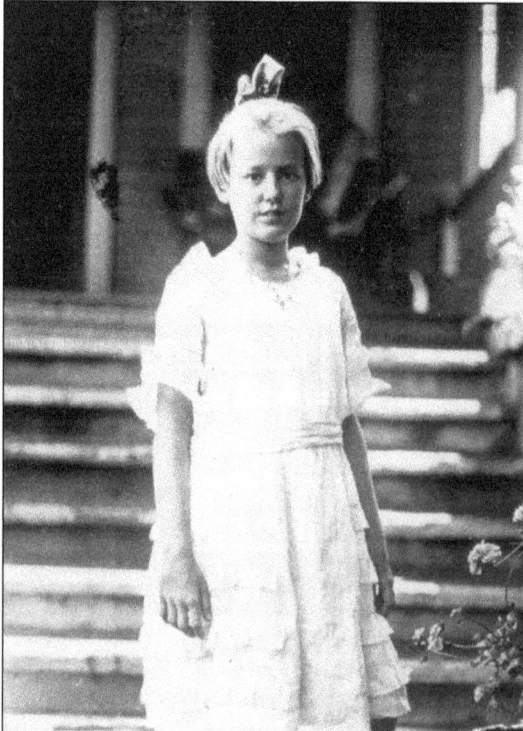

HELEN JANE PERRY. Helen Jane Perry poses on the steps of the Nat T. Perry property in this photograph taken during the early 1900s. (Photograph courtesy of Nancy Jane Earnest and Benjamin F. Earnest Jr.)

HOOVER DAY, OCTOBER 6, 1928.
Elizabethton was decked in red, white,
and blue bunting in anticipation
of presidential candidate Herbert
Hoover's visit to the city. (Photograph
courtesy of the City of Elizabethton.)

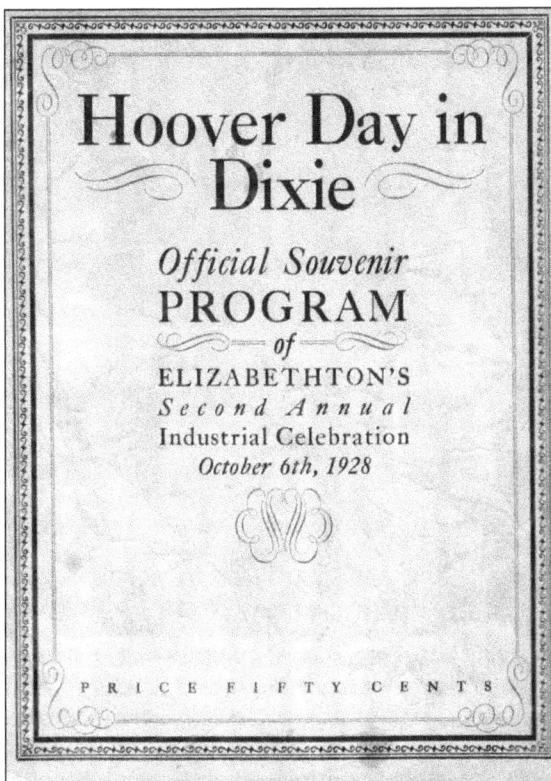

Hoover Day in
Dixie

Official Souvenir
PROGRAM
of
ELIZABETHTON'S
Second Annual
Industrial Celebration
October 6th, 1928

PRICE FIFTY CENTS

HOOVER DAY IN DIXIE. This
program, tied with Bemberg silk,
describes the events held on Hoover
Day when presidential candidate
Herbert Hoover visited Elizabethton
in 1928. (Program courtesy of the City
of Elizabethton.)

HOOVER DAY, OCTOBER 6, 1928. Presidential candidate Herbert Hoover was presented with a key to the city by city manager E.R. Lingerfelt. Trains called "Specials" came from as far away as Knoxville and Roanoke as visitors and residents alike flooded Elizabethton to welcome Mr. and Mrs. Herbert Hoover. (Photograph courtesy of the Herbert Hoover Presidential Library/Museum.)

HOOVER DAY, OCTOBER 6, 1928. School children walk across the "new" Watauga River Bridge on the Bristol Highway, eager to welcome the motorcade of presidential candidate Herbert Hoover to Elizabethton. (Photograph courtesy of the Herbert Hoover Presidential Library/Museum.)

HOOVER DAY, OCTOBER 6, 1928. A luncheon was provided for Mr. and Mrs. Hoover at the Lynnwood Hotel by the Chamber of Commerce. (Photograph courtesy of the Herbert Hoover Presidential Library/Museum.)

HOOVER DAY, OCTOBER 6, 1928. The presidential candidate was given a grand tour of American Bemberg Corporation, one of the industrial giants of Elizabethton, Tennessee that "placed Elizabethton on the industrial map of the New South." (Photograph courtesy of the Herbert Hoover Presidential Library/Museum.)

HOOVER DAY, OCTOBER 6, 1928. Presidential candidate Herbert Hoover and Mrs. Hoover participate in the parade, which traveled down Elk Avenue to the Soldiers' Monument. Originally planned as a show of industrial progress, the parade included several floats that depicted Elizabethton's colorful history. Following the parade, Mr. Hoover delivered his powerful address in Harmon Field. (Photograph courtesy of the Herbert Hoover Presidential Library/Museum.)

FRANKLIN CLUBHOUSE. For many years, the Franklin Club functioned as the social center for the employers of American Bemberg Corporation and American Glanzstoff Corporation (later known as North American Rayon.) The elegant building, which had walls lined with luxurious Bemberg silk, was destroyed by fire in 1980. (Photograph courtesy of Nancy Jane Earnest and Benjamin F. Earnest Jr.)

THE FRANKLIN POOL. Helen Earnest (right) is pictured here at the Franklin Pool. Located near Sycamore Shoals, the pool was another benefit provided for the Bemberg and Glanzstoff family. (Photograph courtesy of Nancy Jane Earnest and Benjamin F. Earnest Jr.)

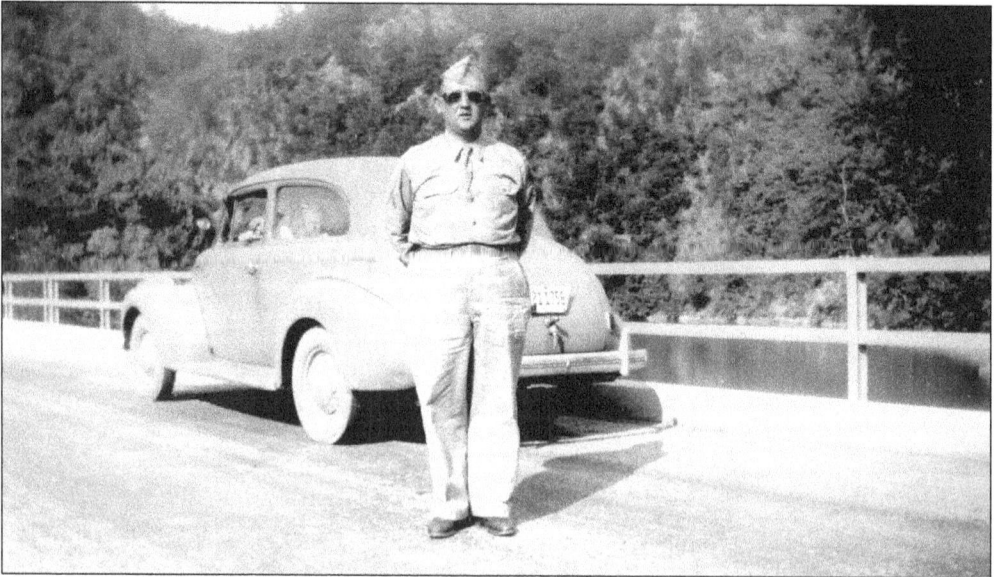

BRIDGE OVER WILBUR LAKE, 1942. Conley H. Estep poses with his children Glen Estep and Mildred Estep on the bridge crossing Wilbur Lake. (Photograph courtesy of Jim and Connie Vaughn.)

VISIT FROM GREER GARSON, 1942. In an effort to encourage the purchase of war bonds, famed movie star Greer Garson visited Elizabethton during a large patriotic rally held September 3, 1942. (Photograph by Herchel E. Ornduff, courtesy of Jeter and Phyllis Hale.)

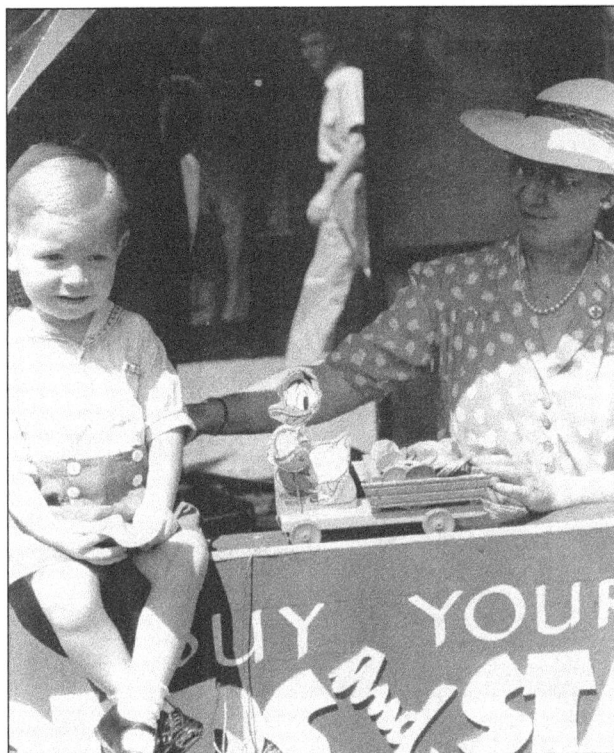

BUYING BONDS, 1942. With a wagon load of 75 silver dollars, Jeter Hale is ready to purchase war bonds. (Photograph by Herchel E. Ornduff, courtesy of Jeter and Phyllis Hale.)

BIKE PARADE ON ELK AVENUE. Photographs of parades may seem commonplace, but upon closer inspection they offer a glimpse of businesses no longer in existence. Notice the variety of businesses represented in this bike parade from the 1940s. (Photograph courtesy of Nancy Jane Earnest and Benjamin F. Earnest Jr.)

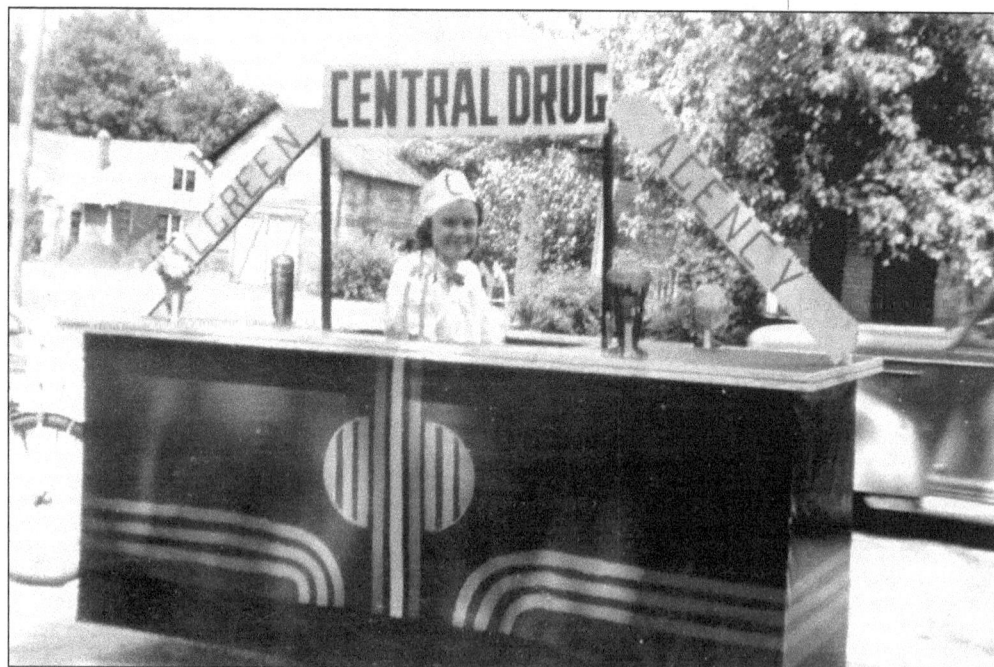

BIKE PARADE ON ELK AVENUE, c. 1940s. Central Drug is represented in the bike parade. (Photograph courtesy of Nancy Jane Earnest and Benjamin F. Earnest Jr.)

BIKE PARADE ON ELK AVENUE, c. 1940S.
Betty Sammons Tony advertises Earnest's
Greenhouse Florist in the bike parade.
(Photograph courtesy of Nancy Jane
Earnest and Benjamin F. Earnest Jr.)

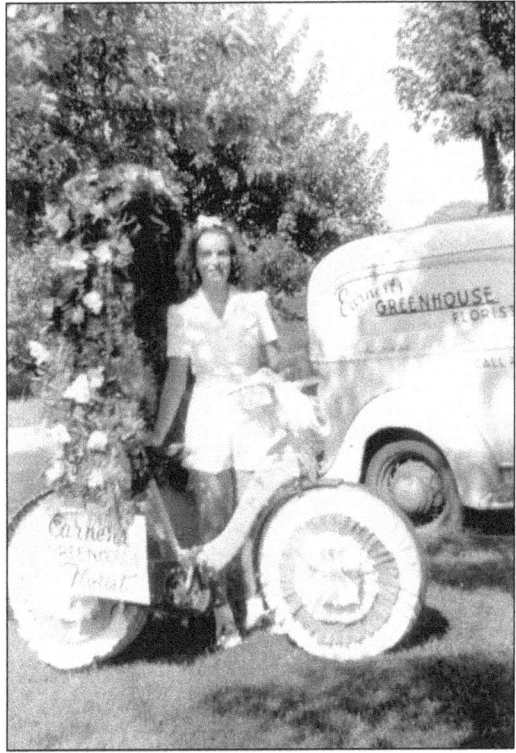

COSTUME PARTY, 1950S. Children dress
up at the preschool of the First United
Methodist Church. (Photograph courtesy
First United Methodist Church.)

THE HONOR ROLL, 1951. Nearly 5,000 veterans were honored on the wooden billboard placed near the Soldiers' Monument in the 1940s. (Photograph from the collection of the late W.G. Ziletti, courtesy of Joe Alexander.)

'54 FORD. Patsy Wallace, Barbara Dugger, Danny McCall, Janice Heaton, Ben Earnest, and Carol Brooks pose in this show car at Carter County Motor Company. (Photograph courtesy of Nancy Jane Earnest and Benjamin F. Earnest Jr.)

ELK AVENUE PARADE, 1959. Duncan Renaldo, better known as "The Cisco Kid," rides in one of many parades down Elk Avenue. (Photograph courtesy of Nancy Jane Earnest and Benjamin F. Earnest Jr.)

ELK AVENUE PARADE, 1959. Industrial giant Bemberg Cupioni is represented in the parade. Notice the presence of Burgie Drugs and Betsy Theatre in the background. (Photograph courtesy of Nancy Jane Earnest and Benjamin F. Earnest Jr.)

ELK AVENUE PARADE, 1959. Nancy Jane Earnest and Tim and Suzie Briscoe enjoy the parade down Elk Avenue. (Photograph courtesy of Nancy Jane Earnest and Benjamin F. Earnest Jr.)

THE LINGERFELT DELIVERY TRUCK. Times have changed, but residents of Elizabethton are still fond of the old cars. This 1931 hard top was owned by Harold Lingerfelt until 1980. (Photograph courtesy of Harold Lingerfelt.)

Four

SCHOOLS, SPORTS, AND CHURCHES

EAST SIDE SCHOOL, 1954. Kenneth Fritts, Janice Steel, and Mr. Campbell handle the American flag at East Side School. (Photograph originally printed in the *Watauga Spinnerette*, January/February 1954.)

CONLEY H. ESTEP AND HATTIE E. HYDER ESTEP, LATE 1930S. Before transportation was provided for students in the Carter County School System, small schools like Tiger Creek and Piney Grove dotted the mountainsides. (Photograph courtesy of Jim and Connie Vaughn.)

KEENBURG ELEMENTARY SCHOOL. Part of the Carter County School System, Keenburg Elementary School began operation in 1901. In 1979, the older section of the school, condemned as a fire hazard during the previous school year, was demolished. (Photograph courtesy of Keenburg Elementary School.)

SOUTHSIDE ELEMENTARY SCHOOL. Southside Elementary School functioned as a Carter County School until July 1985. (Photograph by authors.)

WEST SIDE ELEMENTARY SCHOOL. In 1929, American Bemberg Corporation and American Glanzstoff Corporation provided two houses on Orchard Road to be used for school children living on the west side of town. The present school building was erected in 1953. (Photograph by authors.)

CEDAR STREET, EARLY 1940S. Young Jeter Hale and Charlie Fair are pictured near Cedar Street. (Photograph courtesy of Jeter and Phyllis Hale.)

OLD HAROLD MCCORMICK SCHOOL, 1947. Included in this photograph taken in front of Old Harold McCormick are Jeter Hale, Patsy Buckles, June Chambers, Alice Gass, Carolyn Anderson, Robert Kelly, Wayne Hemby, Janice Deloach, Louise Fair, Harmon Gouge, Jerry Adams, Danny Jenkins, Patsy Jessee, ? Hodge, Kenneth Humphrey, and Glen Hyder. (Photograph courtesy of Jeter and Phyllis Hale.)

EAST SIDE SCHOOL, 1954. East Side School, part of the Elizabethton City School System, was built in 1952. Mrs. W.K. Main served as the school's first principal from 1952 to 1969. (Photograph originally printed in the *Watauga Spinnerette*, January/February 1954.)

OLD T.A. DUGGER SCHOOL. Pictured here is the old campus of T.A. Dugger before the students were moved to the old high school on West E Street in 1974. (Photograph courtesy of Joe and Elaine Hopkins.)

T.A. Dugger Jr. T.A. Dugger Jr., after whom the junior high school was named, served as superintendent of the Elizabethton City School System from 1946 to 1962. (Photograph originally printed in the *Watauga Spinnerette*, January/February 1954.)

Old Elizabethton High School, 1940s. Many businesses were represented at the bike parade as participants line up in front of the old high school. (Photograph courtesy of Nancy Jane Earnest and Benjamin F. Earnest Jr.)

1957 FALL FESTIVAL. "Jeter Presley" performs at the 1957 Fall Festival of the Elizabethton High School. (Photograph courtesy of Jeter and Phyllis Hale.)

ELIZABETHTON HIGH SCHOOL BAND. In 1949, the Elizabethton High School Band won the state championship. (Photograph courtesy of Richard and Phyllis Lovette.)

ELK AVENUE PARADE, 1959. The "Betsy" Band of Elizabethton High School marches down the center of Elk Avenue. (Photograph courtesy of Nancy Jane Earnest and Benjamin F. Earnest Jr.)

"BETSY" BAND, 1984. Notice the presence of the Western Auto and the Dollar General Store in this photograph of the Elizabethton High School band celebrating homecoming. (Photograph courtesy of Joe and Elaine Hopkins.)

TENNESSEE TECHNOLOGY CENTER. In 1963, Tennessee established a statewide system of vocational technical schools to assist in training citizens of Tennessee for work force development in technical skills. This center, the Herman Robinson Vocational Technical School, opened in Elizabethton in 1965 to fulfill that mission. (Photograph by authors.)

TENNESSEE TECHNOLOGY CENTER. In 1994, the state legislature changed the name of the state area vocational technical schools to Tennessee Technology Centers. This new campus, located on Highway 91, was opened in the 1990s. (Photograph by authors.)

NORTHEAST STATE TECHNICAL COMMUNITY COLLEGE. In 1966, Northeast State opened as one of the State Area Vocational Technical Schools. However, Northeast State expanded to meet the growing need in the area for a two-year college with an extended curriculum. Not only did it provide two-year degrees in technical fields, but also added programs in health related areas and a university parallel program for students to transfer to a four-year institution after completion of their course work. Along with these expansions, Northeast State also added more campuses to its system. Seen here is the Elizabethton Campus near the industrial park. (Photograph by authors.)

NAVE CENTER. The Nave Center, located behind Elizabethton High School, is not only an East Tennessee State University campus site of the College of Public and Allied Health, but it also houses the Aphasia Research and Treatment Center of the ETSU Speech-Language and Hearing Clinic. (Photograph by authors.)

MOODY AVIATION. This aerial photograph, taken during the winter of 1969, shows Elizabethton Municipal Airport and the newly completed Moody Aviation. Due to the direct access to the runway, the Elizabethton Airport, opened in September 1967, offered the perfect location for the missionary aviation program of Moody Bible Institute. (Photograph courtesy of Moody Bible Institute.)

MOODY AVIATION. Director Dirk Van Dam and Julian Andersen survey the construction of Moody Aviation, which relocated from Chicago, Illinois, to the mountainous terrain of northeast Tennessee in 1969. (Photograph courtesy of Moody Bible Institute.)

MOODY AVIATION. For more than 30 years, students from Moody Bible Institute in Chicago, Illinois, have completed their training in aviation and avionics at Moody Aviation facility in Elizabethton. (Photograph courtesy of Moody Bible Institute.)

MOODY AVIATION. Since 1949, Moody Aviation has been training men and women to provide air transportation for missionaries identified by Paul Robinson, founder of Moody Aviation, as "workers in isolated, undeveloped areas of the world where the trails are treacherous, the roads practically impassable, or the rivers navigable only by the most primitive means." (Photograph courtesy of Moody Bible Institute.)

MOODY AVIATION. Missionary pilots need to be able to do more than merely fly an aircraft. They must also be able to do all major maintenance on their planes in the most primitive of locations. Pictured here is a student learning how to work on both airframe and power plant. (Photographs courtesy of Moody Bible Institute.)

MOODY AVIATION. This recent photograph of the Elizabethton Municipal Airport and Moody Aviation shows the improvements that have been made through the years, including an extension of the taxi way. (Photograph courtesy of Moody Bible Institute.)

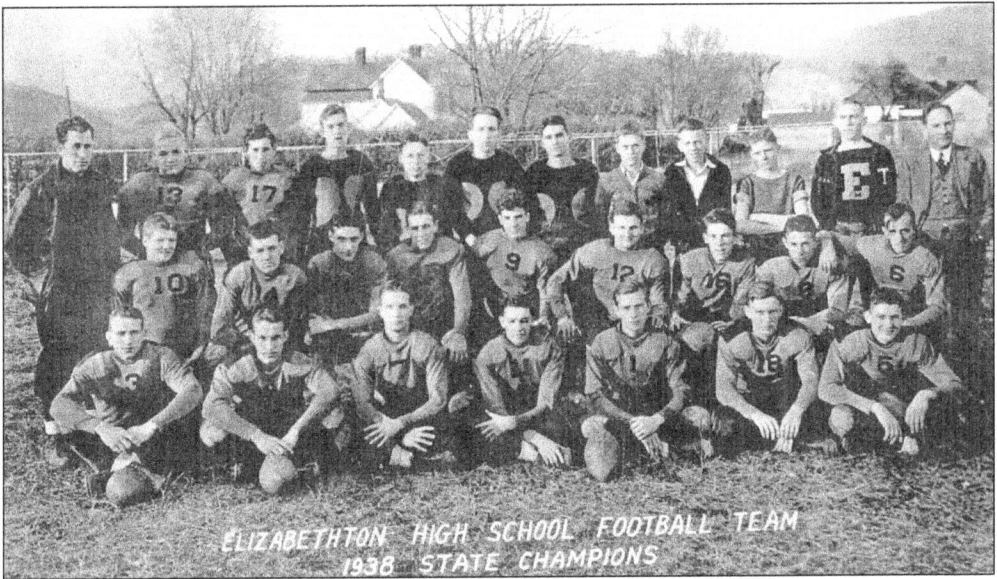

ELIZABETHTON HIGH SCHOOL FOOTBALL, 1938. In 1938, the high school football team won the state championship. The team members that led the school to the victory are, from left to right, the following: (front row) Walter Maupin, Charlie Maupin, Everett Hayes, Bob Givens, Bailey Williams, Ivan Hayes, and Hank Childress; (middle row) John Large, Harold Stevenson, Jess Benton, Walter Lance, Haywood Elliott, Cot Presnell, Bud Hale, John Laws, and James Munsey; (back row) Coach E. Niles Brown, Ed Chambers, Mack Sturgell, Spider Webb, Frank Crockett, John Dance, Ernest Rasar, Zeb Presnell, Harvey Smith, Colyan Parker, Luther Boyd, manager; and T.J. Boswell, assistant coach. (Photograph courtesy of Richard and Phyllis Lovette.)

GIRLS' BASKETBALL SQUAD. The team members of the 1933–1934 girls' basketball squad are, from left to right, the following: (front row) Catherine Chambers, Bernice Clark, Stella Neal, Mary Neal, Marie Hyder, Mae Bowling, Stella Fair, and Fannie Mae Jones; (back row) Anna Mae Pierce, Virginia Thomas, Virginia Hardin, Blonnie Hyder, Bobbie Forrester, Johnnie Parsons, and Mrs. Snell, coach. (Photograph courtesy of Richard and Phyllis Lovette.)

ELIZABETHTON HIGH SCHOOL BASEBALL TEAM. The Red Sox minor league team that made its home in Elizabethton during the 1930s and 1940s donated its uniforms to the high school baseball team. Proudly wearing the "new" uniforms are, from left to right, (front row) Bo Fair, Bill Holden, Phil Ellis, Carroll Broome, Bud Potter, Bob Hankins, and E.C. McQueen; (back row) E. Niles Brown, Coach, unidentified, ? Miller, B. Harold Stout, Pat Spurgeon, W.L. Kimbro, Bill Carter, and unidentified. (Photograph courtesy of Harold Lingerfelt.)

DINO'S TEAM CHAMPIONS. In 1970, the softball team sponsored by Dino's Restaurant won its league's championship. (Photograph courtesy of Dino Senesi.)

THE CARMON DUGGER SPORTS COMPLEX. Home of the Elizabethton Twins, the Carmon Dugger Sports Complex offers an abundant supply of summer entertainment for the whole community. (Photograph courtesy of the Elizabethton Twins.)

KIRBY PUCKETT. During his first year with the Elizabethton Twins, Kirby Puckett batted a .382 average. He went on to play major league ball with the Minnesota Twins in 1984 and was inducted into the Baseball Hall of Fame in 1999. (Photograph courtesy of Dino Senesi.)

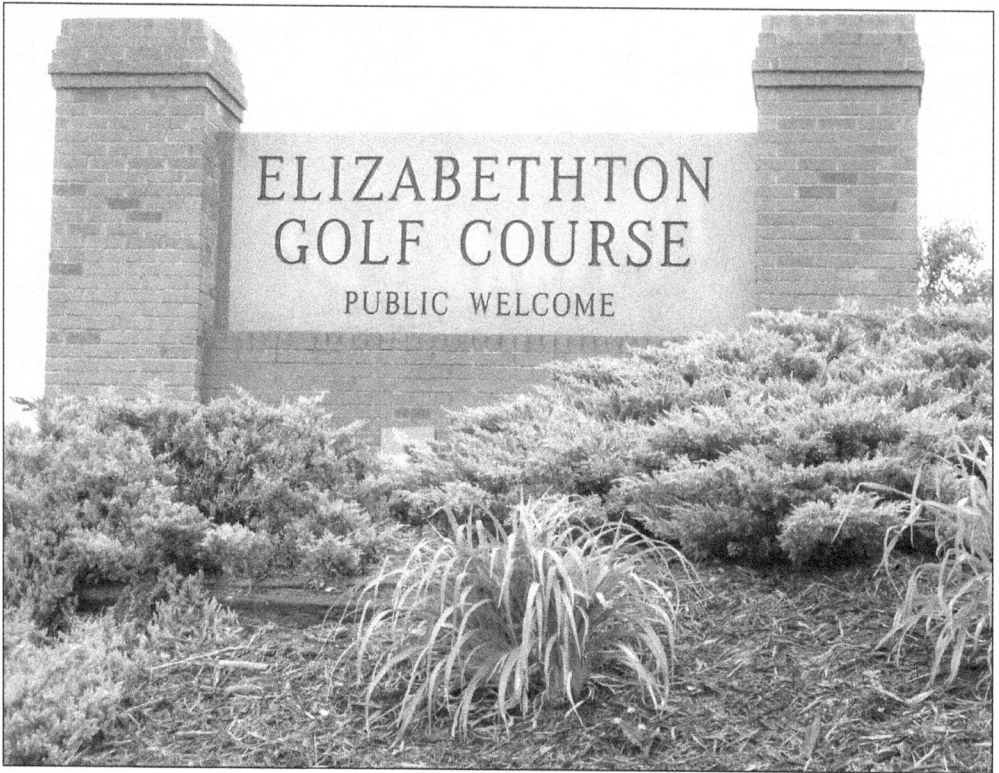

ELIZABETHTON GOLF COURSE. The Elizabethton Golf Course was initially a private endeavor opened in 1936. In 1938, the City of Elizabethton took over the nine-hole course and opened it to the public. In the 1950s, land was purchased to increase the course to a full 18-hole course. (Photographs by authors.)

FIRST PRESBYTERIAN CHURCH. First Presbyterian Church traces its beginnings to 1782, which makes it the oldest church in Elizabethton. During the early 1900s, the church, then located on the corner of Main and Second Streets, opened its doors to a number of area congregations, including the southern branch of the Methodist Church, for short periods of time. First Presbyterian was also instrumental in the development of Davies Academy, a private academy that later became known as Harold McCormick School. (Photograph by authors.)

First Free Will Baptist Church Choir

ELIZABETHTON, TENNESSEE

JOY IN SERVING THE LORD

FIRST FREE WILL BAPTIST CHURCH. The Elizabethton Free Will Baptist Church was organized in 1909 with 22 charter members. In 1913, the building and property on the corner of First and Academy Street was purchased from the northern branch of the Methodist Church for $500. (Photograph by authors.) Below, members of the First Free Will Baptist Church Choir that performed in this 1971 recording are, (left row, front to back) "Bo" Campbell, Lewis Garrison, John R. Campbell, James Pritchard, Dick Hampton, F.D. Elliott, Raymond Lowe, Winford Knode, Rick Knode, and George Lovelace; (middle row) Joann Campbell, Doris Raper, Lois Brown, Judy Williams, Linda Smith, Janet Phillips, Mary Edith Knode, Sue Hampton, Charlotte Lowe, and James Earl Roper, pastor; (right row) Teresa Loudy, Paulette Taylor, Cathy Campbell, Sonja Lowe, Shelia Roper, Rita Bush, Ann Morgan, Kathy Roper, Mary Evelyn Taylor, Katherine Peters, Carol Ann Bowers, and John Holder. (Record Album courtesy of Joe Coffman.)

HARVEST BAPTIST CHURCH. The building now housing Harvest Baptist Church has, in the past, been the meeting place of several congregations including Singletary Memorial Methodist and the Lighthouse for Jesus. (Photograph by authors.)

ST. ELIZABETH CATHOLIC CHURCH. Since its origin in 1923, the St. Elizabeth Catholic Church met in several different homes and even at one time in the Old Governor Taylor Hotel, before members built their present building on C Street in 1949. In 1935, the church started a parochial school, which operated for nearly 20 years. (Photograph by authors.)

OAK STREET BAPTIST CHURCH. The Oak Street Baptist Church, a mission of First Baptist Church, met at a number of places including the Stateline Depot, the old bottling works building, and the Davis Building before erecting this building on Oak Street in 1938. (Photograph courtesy of Lois Milhorn.)

OAK STREET BAPTIST CHURCH. In 1992, Oak Street Baptist Church built a larger sanctuary to house its growing congregation. (Photograph courtesy of Lois Milhorn.)

94

REDEEMER LUTHERAN CHURCH. Located on F Street, the Redeemer Lutheran Church began ministering to the community in 1937. (Photograph by authors.)

FIRST BAPTIST CHURCH. The first building of First Baptist Church was built at the intersection of Broad and Main Streets in 1892. Following the flood in 1901, the church building was moved to Sycamore Street and Elk Avenue in New Town. J.H. Hyder, pastor of First Baptist Church, served the congregation from 1881 to 1883. (Photographs courtesy of First Baptist Church.)

95

First Baptist Church. Pictured here are the members of the First Baptist Church in the 1890s. (Photograph courtesy of First Baptist Church.)

First Baptist Church, 1922. The Baraca Sunday School class poses in front of the church with the teacher, J.C. Price, and president, J.B. Moore. The building located at Sycamore Street and Elk Avenue underwent several changes and additions due to the continued growth in the church. (Photograph courtesy of First Baptist Church.)

FIRST BAPTIST CHURCH. In 1925, the Nat T. Perry property, located on Sunset Hill in New Town Elizabethton, was purchased by the First Baptist Church. On Mother's Day, 1934, the entire congregation posed with the pastor Dr. Bowden in front of the new building located at F Street and Lynn Avenue. (Photograph courtesy of First Baptist Church.)

FIRST BAPTIST CHURCH. The members of the Silent Class of First Baptist Church were, from left to right, the following: (front row) Margaret Campbell, John Campbell Jr., John Campbell Sr., Franklin Bowden Campbell, Mrs. Bessie Campbell, and Josephine Campbell; (back row) Otis Jackson, John F. Crumley, General Moreland, Sam Butner, and Games Spitzer. (Photograph courtesy of First Baptist Church.)

ST. THOMAS' EPISCOPAL
CHURCH, 1950S. Originally
named Calvary Episcopal
Church, St. Thomas' Episcopal
Church was founded in 1892.
(Photograph courtesy of St.
Thomas' Episcopal Church.)

ST. THOMAS' EPISCOPAL
CHURCH. The children's
Sunday school class poses
on the steps of St. Thomas'
Episcopal Church in this
photograph taken in the 1930s.
(Photograph courtesy of St.
Thomas' Episcopal Church.)

St. Thomas' Episcopal Church. The sanctuary of St. Thomas' Episcopal Church is seen as it appeared prior to the fire in 1988. (Photograph courtesy of St. Thomas' Episcopal Church.)

First United Methodist Church. After years of separation caused by the Civil War, Central Methodist Church (the southern branch) and Memorial Methodist Church (the northern branch) reunited in 1944. The church, then known as First Methodist, worshipped at the sanctuary on the corner of E and Elm Street. In 1968, the name changed to United Methodist Church when the two denominations—the Methodists and the Evangelical United Brethren—merged. (Photograph courtesy of First United Methodist Church.)

FIRST UNITED METHODIST CHURCH, 1950S. Once reunited, the church purchased adjacent property and constructed an educational building in 1948. Pictured here is the men's Sunday school class that met in the basement of that building. (Photograph courtesy of First United Methodist Church.)

ALICE DUNGAN SUNDAY SCHOOL CLASS, c. 1941. The ladies of First United Methodist Church met for a quilting party at the home of Mrs. J.A. Clear. From left to right are (seated) Mrs. Finley Richards, unidentified, and Mrs. Vance; (standing) Mrs. George Ryan, Mrs. Clark, Mrs. Large, Mrs. Walter Hodge, Mrs. Dave Wetzel, Mrs. S.G. Geisler, Mrs. T.J. Mims, Mrs. Gus Crumley, Mrs. Boring, and Mrs. J.A. Clear. (Photograph courtesy of First United Methodist Church.)

100

ELIZABETHTON ALLIANCE CHURCH. The Elizabethton Alliance Church, formally organized in 1988, met in several places, including the old bus station, before permanently moving into the vacant Parks-Belk building in 1991. Pictured below are the charter members of the church meeting in the bus station. (Photographs courtesy of Joe and Elaine Hopkins.)

ELIZABETHTON ALLIANCE CHURCH. Pictured here on Promotion Sunday, August 24, 1997, from left to right, are (front row) Lydia Bruce, Asa Murley, Rose Presnell, Rebekah Wiedenfeld, and Stephen Wiedenfeld; (middle row) Sarah Hayter, Seth Bruce, Lyndsie Yontz, Lydia Depew, and Hannah Wiedenfeld; (back row) April Burwick, Erin Babb, Amber Bruce, Alía Robinson, Johnny McMeen, and Isaac Williams. (Photograph courtesy of Elizabethton Alliance Church.)

ELIZABETHTON ALLIANCE CHURCH. Michael Depew teaches *Genesis* to one of the adult Sunday school classes in 1996. (Photograph courtesy of Elizabethton Alliance Church.)

Five

MUNICIPAL

THE OLD HUNTER HOME. Located at the corner of Watauga and G Streets, the Old Hunter Home housed several different entities, including the Elizabethton General Hospital from 1920 to 1928, the Doctor's Hospital organized by J.B. Shoun, the Lutheran Church, the Elizabethton Public Library, and the American Legion. (Photograph courtesy of Ann Moody.)

THE OLD MUNICIPAL BUILDING. Built in 1927, the old municipal building was the site of the city government for 62 years before being leveled in November 1990. (Photograph courtesy of the City of Elizabethton.)

DAYTON HUNTER. Dayton Hunter, the first city manager of Elizabethton, served the city from August 17, 1922 to March 15, 1923. Hunter was instrumental in the establishment of Wilbur Dam, the first dam with a hydro-electric power plant in Tennessee. (Photograph courtesy of the City of Elizabethton.)

E.C. ALEXANDER. Edwin Crawford Alexander, son of Dr. James Alexander, served the city of Elizabethton as the fifth city manager from November 14, 1933 to October 19, 1936, and as the seventh city manager from May 20, 1937 to May 4, 1945. During the course of his illustrious career, Mr. Alexander was instrumental in bringing American Bemberg Corporation and American Glanzstoff Corporation to the area. (Photograph courtesy of the City of Elizabethton.)

Wishing You a Merry Christmas and a Happy New Year

Dr. and Mrs. John B. Shoun

DR. SHOUN'S HOSPITAL
ELIZABETHTON. TENN.

CHRISTMAS POSTCARD ADVERTISING DR. SHOUN'S HOSPITAL. Dr. John B. Shoun practiced medicine in Elizabethton for several years. (Postcard courtesy of Dino's Restaurant.)

ST. ELIZABETH HOSPITAL. Both St. Elizabeth Hospital and Franklin Clinic served the needs of Elizabethton until the Carter County Memorial Hospital opened in 1959. The St. Elizabeth Hospital, organized by doctors J.O. Wood, W.C. Caudill, E.L. Caudill, and Charles Baughman, began operation in 1927. (Photograph by authors.)

FRANKLIN CLINIC. The Franklin Clinic, organized by Drs. E.T. Pearson, A.E. Miller, H.B Dameron, and Leslie Herd, began operation in 1947. (Photograph by authors.)

CARTER COUNTY MEMORIAL HOSPITAL. In 1952, Elizabethton became eligible to obtain funding under the Hill-Burton Act. Residents of the city and county received care at the Carter County Memorial Hospital from 1959 to 1986. (Photograph by authors.)

SYCAMORE SHOALS HOSPITAL. Sycamore Shoals Hospital has provided for the healthcare needs of Elizabethton and Carter County since 1986. (Photograph courtesy of the Mountain States Health Alliance.)

ELIZABETHTON POST OFFICE, SYCAMORE STREET. The Elizabethton Post Office operated at the Sycamore Street site from 1932 to 1988 before moving to West Elk Avenue. (Photograph courtesy of the Elizabethton Post Office.)

ELIZABETHTON SANITARY DEPARTMENT. Members of the city council pose with the sanitary department and its new truck. (Photograph courtesy of the City of Elizabethton.)

PLEASANT ANDREW JACKSON CROCKETT. The Carter County Sheriff Department, established in 1796, fulfilled all of the law enforcement duties for Carter County as well as the City of Elizabethton until the establishment of the Elizabethton Police Department in 1905. Pleasant Andrew Jackson Crockett, grandfather of Attorney Charles Crockett and great grandfather of Attorney David Crockett, served as sheriff from 1865 to 1866. (Photograph courtesy of the Carter County Sheriff's Department.)

MILLARD (JIM) MORELAND
ELECTED
SHERIFF OF CARTER COUNTY
1926 - 1930

MILLARD "JIM" MORELAND. Millard "Jim" Moreland served as sheriff from 1926 to 1930 and from 1932 to 1938. During his tenure as sheriff, it is reputed that Sheriff Moreland sent his family away and slept on his roof due to death threats resulting from his crackdown on "bootlegging" and "moonshining" in the area. (Photograph courtesy of the Carter County Sheriff's Department.)

GEORGE PAPANTONIOU. George Papantoniou, who served as sheriff from 1976 to 1982, poses with the men of the Carter County Sheriff's Department. (Photograph courtesy of Joe Coffman.)

CHIEF EVANS COLLINS. The Elizabethton Police Department was established in 1905 with Chief Evans Collins serving as Elizabethton's first town marshall. (Photograph courtesy of the Elizabethton Police Department.)

ELIZABETHTON POLICE DEPARTMENT. Speed patrolman Patrick "Pat" Henry Ingoldsby (second row, left side) stands among these fine officers in a photograph taken between 1931 and 1934. (Photograph courtesy of the Elizabethton Police Department.)

CHIEF TOM CARRIGER. Tom Carriger served the city of Elizabethton as the first chief of police when Elizabethton changed from a town marshall system to a city police department. (Photograph courtesy of the Elizabethton Police Department.)

111

ELIZABETHTON POLICE DEPARTMENT. Pictured with Chief of Police Mike Boatright (left) are Gus Crumley, Tom Banner, John DeVault, Gene Holly, Sam Elliott, Claude Nave (future chief of police), and Jim "Dude" Lipford. Boatright also served as the sheriff of Carter County from 1942 to 1944 and 1954 to 1960. (Photograph courtesy of the Elizabethton Police Department.)

ELIZABETHTON POLICE DEPARTMENT. Elizabethton Police "meterman" J.W. Spangler parks the city's new 1969 Harley-Davidson motor tricycle on Sycamore Street. (Photograph courtesy of the Elizabethton Police Department.)

K-9 SERGEANT SAM. In 1992, the Elizabethton Police Department established the first K-9 units to serve the city of Elizabethton. K-9 Sergeant Sam, pictured with Officer Charlie Moreland, served for six years on the Elizabethton Police Force. (Photograph courtesy of the Elizabethton Police Department.)

K-9 SERGEANT MAX. Pictured here with Officer Carl Burrough, K-9 Sergeant Max served for five years. Both Max and Sam were USPCA certified and received basic and narcotic training. (Photograph courtesy of the Elizabethton Police Department.)

ELIZABETHTON FIRE DEPARTMENT. The Elizabethton Fire Department was established in 1905. Chief Walter Dunlap, the first fire chief, was the grandfather of Elizabethton resident Steve Dunlap. (Photograph courtesy of the Elizabethton Fire Department.)

ELIZABETHTON FIRE DEPARTMENT. The Elizabethton Fire Department remained a volunteer department until the 1930s. (Photograph courtesy of the Elizabethton Fire Department.)

ELIZABETHTON FIRE DEPARTMENT. Chief Mark Fletcher was the second chief of the Elizabethton Fire Department. (Photograph courtesy of the Elizabethton Fire Department.)

ELIZABETHTON FIRE DEPARTMENT. Chief Dennis Younce poses with the firefighters at Central Fire Hall in this 1971 photograph. (Photograph courtesy of the Elizabethton Fire Department.)

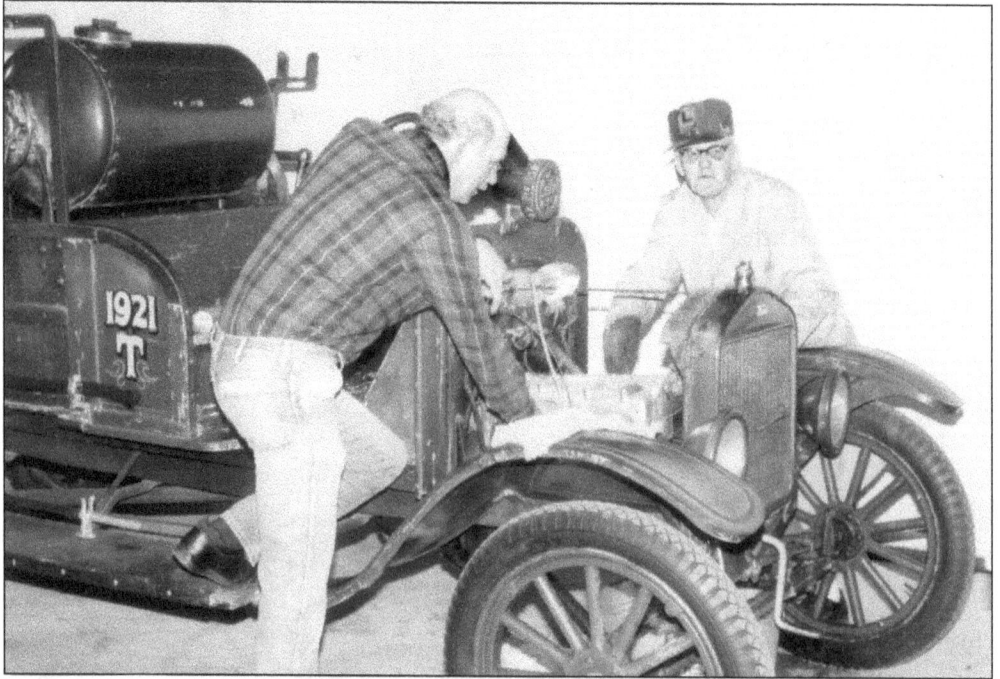

MODEL T FIRE ENGINE. Steve Dunlap and Dale Smith are two of many who restored the 1923 T Model fire engine. (Photograph courtesy of the Elizabethton Fire Department.)

ELIZABETHTON FIRE DEPARTMENT. Steve Dunlap drives the 1923 T Model fire engine with his son Eric. (Photograph courtesy of the Elizabethton Fire Department.)

1923 MODEL T FIRE ENGINE. Restored to its mint condition in 1993–1994, the Model T is on display at the central station of the Elizabethton Fire Department. (Photograph courtesy of the Elizabethton Fire Department.)

STATION #2. As Elizabethton grew, so did the fire department. Station #2, located on G Street, was built in 1970. (Photograph courtesy of the Elizabethton Fire Department.)

STATION #3. Station #3, located across the street from the Elizabethton Golf Course on Buck Van Huss Road, was built in 1997. (Photograph courtesy of the Elizabethton Fire Department.)

118

AMERICAN BEMBERG FIRE. The fire at American Bemberg Corporation in 1981 completely destroyed the facility's west wing. (Photograph courtesy of the Elizabethton Fire Department.)

NORTH AMERICAN RAYON FIRE. Fire departments from as far as Morristown came to Elizabethton to fight the fire at North American Rayon in February 2000. (Photograph courtesy of the Elizabethton Fire Department.)

119

NORTH AMERICAN RAYON FIRE. Capt. Tim Edwards checks supply lines at the North American Rayon Fire. (Photograph courtesy of the Elizabethton Fire Department.)

Six

HISTORIC LANDMARKS

FORT WATAUGA AT SYCAMORE SHOALS. This replica of Fort Watauga was built in 1976 for the bicentennial celebration. The fort was built to the dimensions of the original site located near Gap Creek Road based on an archeological dig in 1975 by the Bicentennial Historical Commission. (Photograph from the collection of the late W.G. Ziletti, courtesy of Joe Alexander.)

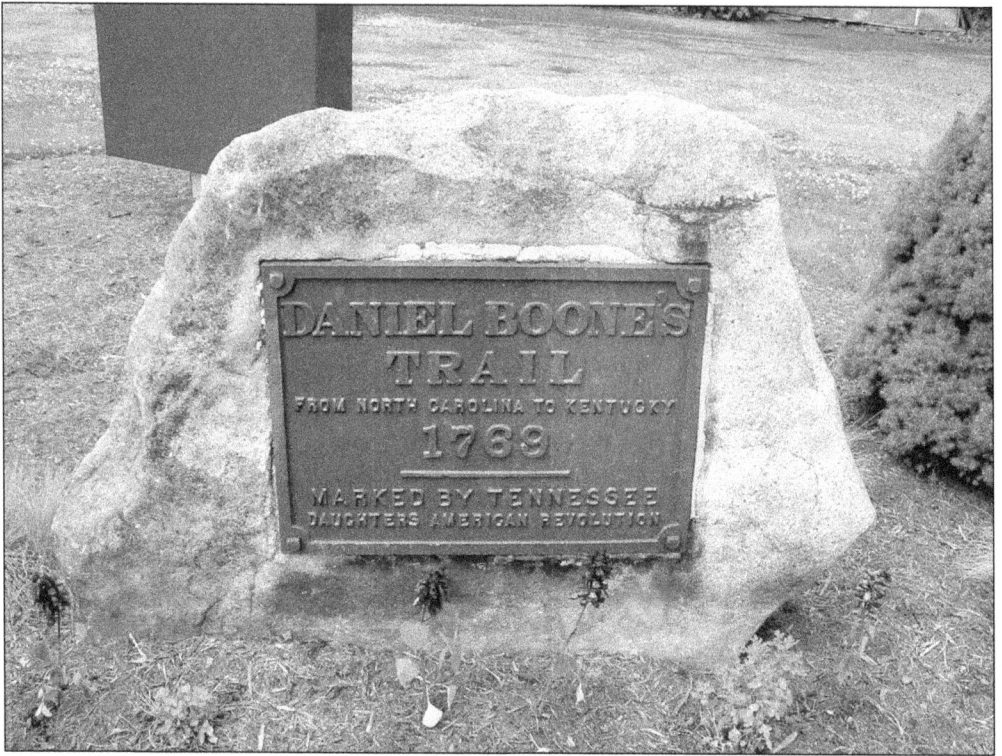

DANIEL BOONE TRAIL MARKER. The Daniel Boone Trail Marker stands to commemorate the historic trail blazed from North Carolina to Kentucky by Daniel Boone that would become the conduit through which western expansion was accomplished. In 1926, the marker was moved from the Bristol Pike to the lawn of the Elizabethton Methodist Episcopal Church by the John Carter Chapter of the Daughters of the American Revolution. (Photograph by authors.)

FORT WATAUGA MONUMENT. This monument, located on West G Street, was unveiled on June 14, 1910 to commemorate Fort Watauga at Sycamore Shoals by the John Sevier, Bonnie Kate, and Sycamore Shoals Chapters of the Daughters of the American Revolution. While the colonies were declaring their independence from England during the summer of 1776, Fort Watauga protected the Wataugans during a two-week siege led by Cherokee chief Old Abram and his band of warriors. The monument is constructed of Tennessee marble and Watauga River rock. (Photograph by authors.)

SYCAMORE SHOALS STATE HISTORIC AREA. Designated as a national historic landmark in the 1970s, Sycamore Shoals State Historic Area provides a wide variety of historic and educational opportunities for young and old alike. (Photograph by authors.)

OVERMOUNTAIN MEN. This bronze statue, fashioned by Jon Mark Estep, immortalizes the frontier spirit of the heroes of the Watauga settlement, who were otherwise known as the Overmountain Men. On September 25, 1780, the Overmountain Men mustered together at Fort Watauga before defeating British Major Patrick Ferguson and his army of Tories at the Battle of King's Mountain in South Carolina. (Photograph by authors.)

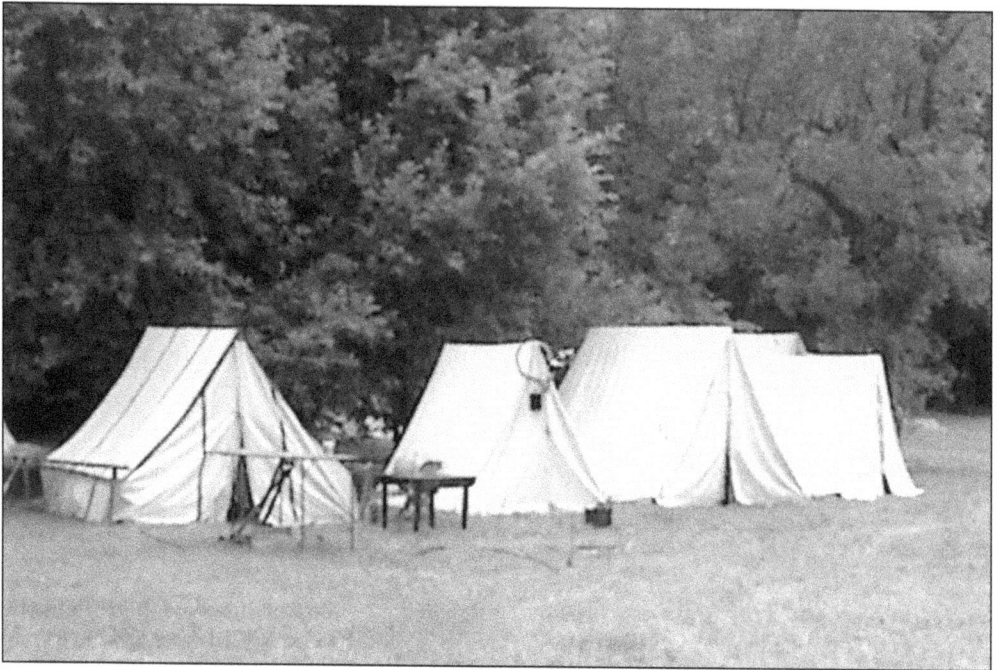

MUSTER AT FORT WATAUGA Each year in May, re-enactors set up living history camps at Sycamore Shoals State Park depicting the muster of the Overmountain Men at Fort Watauga before their long trip to King's Mountain. The tents in this photograph are supplied with 18th-century weaponry, cookware, tools, and bedding. (Photograph by authors.)

MUSTER AT FORT WATAUGA. These re-enactors go to great lengths to dress in 18th-century attire while using speech and mannerisms consistent with the time period. Pictured here are Chad Bogart and Cheryl Smith, dedicated interpreters who volunteer many hours to the living history sites in Elizabethton and Johnson City. (Photograph by authors.)

THE DEPEW CHILDREN. Many of the re-enactors who participate in the living histories at Sycamore Shoals State Park are direct descendants of the Wataugans and the Overmountain Men. Pictured here are (clockwise) Lydia, Priscilla, Isaac, Leo, and John Depew posing in front of a cabin at Fort Watauga. The children are descendants of Isaac Depew, who fought at the Battle of King's Mountain. (Photograph by authors.)

THE WATAUGANS. *The Wataugans*, the official outdoor drama of Tennessee, is held each year during the final three weekends in July. Written by Dr. Ronnie Day and directed by Jon Ruetz, *The Wataugans* have successfully entertained the community for more than 25 years. (Photograph courtesy of Elizabeth and Emma Lee Price.)

MUSKET DEMONSTRATION. Educational services are a primary feature of Sycamore Shoals State Park. Re-enactor Chad Bogart demonstrates to visitors how to prime, load, and fire a flint-lock musket. (Photograph by authors.)

SABINE HALL. Built in 1812 by Gen. Nathaniel Taylor and his wife, Mary Patton Taylor, Sabine Hall on Sabine Hill stands as a firm testimony of days gone by. The Taylors were the great-grandparents of Bob and Alf Taylor, governors of Tennessee. (Photograph by authors.)

TIME CAPSULE. In celebration of the bicentennial of Elizabethton in 1999, a time capsule filled with local memorabilia was buried in the Betsy Walkway to be opened in the year 2099. (Photograph by authors.)

ELIZABETHTON DOWNTOWN. Times have changed, industries, businesses, and families have come and gone, yet Elizabethton has continued to develop into the city planned so long ago. (Photograph by authors.)

THE QUEEN OF THE DOE. For 122 years, the Doe River Covered Bridge has stood the test of time—closing only twice to vehicular traffic for repair. The structure, which has enabled Elizabethton to grow into the city it is today, stands as a monument continually representing the fortitude of the citizens of Elizabethton and Carter County. (Photograph courtesy of Johnny Holder.)

Visit us at
arcadiapublishing.com